OXFORD
RAILWAYS
IN OLD PHOTOGRAPHS
A SECOND SELECTION

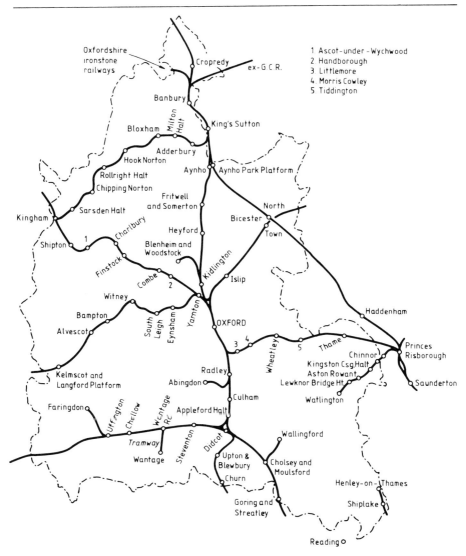

MAP showing the lines covered in this book.

OXFORDSHIRE RAILWAYS

IN OLD PHOTOGRAPHS
A SECOND SELECTION

COLLECTED BY

LAURENCE WATERS

ALAN SUTTON

Alan Sutton Publishing
Phoenix Mill · Far Thrupp · Stroud · Gloucestershire

First published 1991
Reprinted 1997
Copyright © 1991 Laurence Waters

British Library Cataloguing in Publication Data

Oxfordshire railways in old photographs:
a second selection.
I. Waters, Laurence
385.094257

ISBN 0-86299-852-2

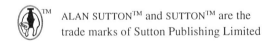
Typeset in 9/10 Korinna.
Typesetting and origination by
Alan Sutton Publishing Limited.
Printed in Great Britain by
The Bath Press, Avon.

CONTENTS

INTRODUCTION

In this second volume of old photographs of Oxfordshire railways I have again used the 'new' Oxfordshire of 1974 as my boundary line. The compilation of a second selection has allowed me to fill in some of the gaps left by the first and also to cover some of the lines in greater detail. Details of opening and closure dates of lines and stations in Oxfordshire can be found in the first book and I have purposely excluded them from this volume to allow for the inclusion of more photographs. In answer to many requests I have also included more pictures of the local industrial lines.

It is now two years since I compiled the first book and in that time the railway network in the county has seen several changes. On the plus side Network South East opened a brand new station at Islip in May 1989, and during 1990 they also rebuilt the station at Oxford. Already the old structure is but a memory and I have included a picture taken just prior to its demolition. On the debit side the oil terminal at Thame closed during March 1991 leaving the future of this line in some doubt. The same might be said about the branch to Chinnor where services to the cement works have now been withdrawn. The future of this line could well be ensured, however, with the formation of the Princes Risborough and Chinnor Railway Preservation Society. The aim of the society is to preserve the line and eventually operate steam passenger services between Risborough and Chinnor. One hopes they succeed.

In conclusion I once again hope that the pictures contained within the following pages will give you as much pleasure as their selection has given me.

I am grateful to those persons who took the trouble to write to me regarding a few errors that crept into volume one: p. 9 the 4–4–0 is 'City' class No. 3717 *City of Winchester*; p. 87 the picture captions should be reversed.

<u>SECTION ONE</u>

Shrivenham to Didcot

THIS VIEW OF SHRIVENHAM was taken in around 1934, shortly after the widening of the tracks.
(Author's Collection)

A 'CASTLE' hurries through Shrivenham with a service to Paddington in around 1960. Note the wonderful ex-broad gauge goods shed. (BR)

'HALL' CLASS 4–6–0 NO. 5978 *Bodinnick Hall* arrives at Uffington with an 'Up' stopping service on 16 May 1959. The platform for the closed Faringdon branch is behind the signal box. (Great Western Trust/M. Hale)

CHALLOW STATION in around 1919. (Oxfordshire County Libraries)

THIS VIEW OF CHALLOW was taken on 17 April 1934 and shows the newly completed four track layout. (Author's Collection)

CHALLOW STATION IMPROVEMENTS. This view, taken on 8 April 1932, shows the new 'Down' platform under construction. (British Railways)

THE UNUSUAL SIGHT of old and new signal boxes at Wantage Road, pictured here in October 1932. The old box in the foreground was removed to allow for track widening. Its replacement can be seen in the background. (British Railways)

WANTAGE ROAD STATION pictured shortly after the 1934 track widening. (Author's Collection)

'KING' CLASS 4–6–0 NO. 6023 *King Edward II* speeds through Wantage Road with a Cardiff to Paddington service in the summer of 1961. The engine survived the cutter's torch and is now kept at Didcot Railway Centre where it is to be restored to working order. (W. Turner)

AN UNIDENTIFIED 4300 CLASS MOGUL runs through Steventon on a summer day in 1931. (Author's Collection)

STEVENTON STATION in around 1910. (Author's Collection)

A LONG MIXED GOODS SERVICE from Severn Tunnel Yard to Reading, hauled by 2–8–0 No. 2899, trundles through Steventon on a summer day in 1961. (W. Turner)

THIS SECOND VIEW OF STEVENTON was taken in May 1952. The large house in the background was constructed by the Great Western for the station superintendent and was used as the company's headquarters between July 1842 and January 1843. (Great Western Trust/M. Hale)

A TREHERBERT TO PADDINGTON EXCURSION TRAIN was derailed at Milton near Didcot on 22 November 1955 killing 11 passengers and injuring 157 others. The engine involved was Britannia Pacific No. 70026 *Polar Star* which fell down the embankment making retrieval difficult. In this first picture, taken on 28 November 1955, the area around the locomotive is being cleared.

PREPARATIONS ARE IN HAND for retrieving the locomotive by 4 December 1955. This required the laying of a special track from the nearby Milton Ordnance depot.

THE LOCOMOTIVE IS RIGHTED . . .

. . . AND IS FINALLY TOWED AWAY BY 0–6–0 3212. (British Railways)

18

DIDCOT JUNCTION on Friday 20 May 1892, with the last 'Down' broad gauge service, the 5 p.m. Paddington to Plymouth, passing through. It is hauled by Gooch 'Iron Duke' class *Bulkeley*. (Author's Collection)

ONE OF GOOCH'S SUPERB BROAD GAUGE 'IRON DUKE' CLASS 4–2–2s *Great Western* stands at Didcot with a 'Down' service in around 1889. Note the engine cleaner's finish on the frames, cab and tender; this was known as 'quivering' and was obtained by rubbing tallow on the paintwork. (Author's Collection)

THIS INTERESTING PICTURE, taken in July 1905, shows the newly constructed signal box at Didcot North Junction. The box was the first power operated box on the Great Western, being fitted with a Siemans-Halske 38 lever electronic frame. The small battery cabin can be seen to the left. (Author's Collection)

MEMBERS OF THE TRAFFIC SECTION pose for the camera at Didcot Ordnance depot in May 1917. Note the Great Western pannier tank fitted with a spark arresting chimney for ordnance depot shunting. (Great Western Trust)

AN UNIDENTIFIED 'SAINT' CLASS 4–6–0 stands at the 'Down' platform at Didcot with a service to the West of England, c. 1928. (Author's Collection)

A GREAT WESTERN RAILWAY MOTOR BUS at Didcot station forecourt, c. 1920. (Author's Collection)

THE STATION APPROACH AT DIDCOT, C. 1920. (Author's Collection)

THE REMAINS OF THE 'DOWN' PLATFORM AT DIDCOT JUNCTION after the fire of 11 March 1886. The station had only just been rebuilt. (Author's Collection)

SOME OF THE STAFF of the Great Western horse provender store at Didcot, c. 1910. (H.D. Cullen)

THE INTERIOR of the horse provender store at Didcot. (Author's Collection)

THE EXTERIOR OF THE HORSE PROVENDER STORES at Didcot, c. 1910. In this large building fodder was made up for the many horses that were used by the Great Western Railway. The building fell out of use in the early 1950s and was eventually demolished in 1967. The site is now Didcot Parkway car park. (Author's Collection)

THE NEWBURY BAY AT DIDCOT photographed on 16 April 1934 to show the recently completed reconstruction work. (British Railways)

DIDCOT STATION in 1932, soon after the start of reconstruction work. Of particular interest is the original engine shed in the centre. (British Railways)

THE BRAND NEW SIGNAL BOX at Didcot Foxhall Junction in December 1931. It was closed with the introduction of MAS in May 1965. (Author's Collection)

THE SIGNAL BOX at Foxhall Junction, Didcot in August 1965. The large horse provender store, out of use by this time, can be seen in centre background. (Great Western Trust/M. Hale)

BR STANDARD CLASS 4 NO. 75052 passes the wartime constructed sidings at Port Meadow with a service to Bletchley. (J.D. Edwards)

'CASTLE' CLASS NO. 7037 *Swindon* awaits departure from Didcot with a stopping service from Swindon to Reading and Paddington. (Derek Tuck)

ON THE MORNING of 14 August 1964 ex-LMS 8F No. 48734, working light engine, collided with a Fawley to Bromford Bridge oil train at Didcot North Junction. The 8F was severely damaged in the fire, as can be seen from this picture of the locomotive standing at Didcot MPD just a few days after the accident. (D. Tuck)

THE REMAINS OF THE FOOTBRIDGE at Didcot North Junction pictured soon after the oil train fire of 14 August 1964. (D. Tuck)

THIS HISTORIC PICTURE shows 2–6–2T No. 6106 shortly after arrival at Didcot on 4 November 1967. No. 6106 was the first Great Western Society engine to arrive at what has now become Didcot Railway Centre. (Great Western Society)

MEMBERS of the RCTS, the Great Western Society and the Oxford University Railway Society pose by the broad gauge replica locomotive *Iron Duke* at Didcot Railway Centre in 1986. The gathering was the occasion of a commemorative dinner to honour David Mather (on footplate) on the occasion of his transfer from Area Manager (Oxford) to Provincial Services Manager (South West). (Author's Collection)

SECTION TWO

Didcot to Oxford

THE AFTERMATH OF A COLLISION between a Paddington to Birkenhead express and a Swindon to Bordesley goods train at Appleford crossing on 13 November 1942. (Author's Collection)

THE NEWLY CONSTRUCTED SIGNAL BOX at Appleford Crossing pictured on 12 November 1952. The original box had been demolished by a goods train on 25 September of the same year. (Author's Collection)

APART FROM THE PAGODA-STYLE WAITING SHELTERS no facilities were provided at Appleford Halt. As the sign informs, tickets had to be obtained from the village post office. (D. Tuck)

THIS VIEW OF THE STATION AT CULHAM is undated but notice the man on the left with his donkey and cart. (Author's Collection)

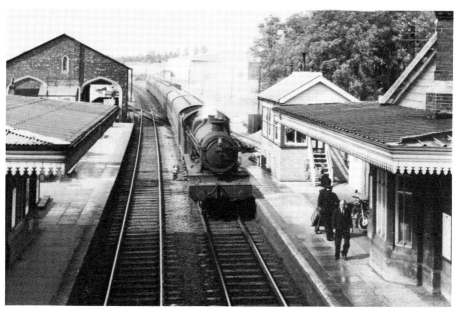
'HALL' CLASS NO. 5983 *Henley Hall* arrives at Culham with a stopping service from Oxford to Reading in around 1958. The small building on the 'Up' platform (right) is a listed Brunel designed structure and still survives. (J.D. Edwards)

THIS EARLY LITHOGRAPH supposedly shows a service from Didcot Junction to Oxford arriving at Abingdon Road Station around 1846. The road here originally crossed the railway on the flat and the turnpike house can be seen in the centre. (Author's Collection)

'HALL' CLASS NO. 4977 *Watcombe Hall* crosses the river bridge at Nuneham with an 'Up' freight service on 28 April 1956. (D. Hall)

RADLEY STATION AND SIGNAL BOX, c. 1919. (Oxfordshire County Libraries)

RADLEY STATION LOOKING SOUTH on 27 February 1959. 'Grange' class No. 6851 *Hurst Grange* leaves for Oxford with a stopping service from Reading. The Abingdon branch bay can be seen on the right. (J.D. Edwards)

THE CREW of 0–6–0 pannier tank No. 1996 pose for the photographer at Radley on 2 January 1912. (Author's Collection)

THIS VIEW OF KENNINGTON JUNCTION SIGNAL BOX was taken in the winter of 1912. (Author's Collection)

0–4–2T NO. 1444 waits in the goods loop at Kennington Junction with an Abingdon to Hinksey yard goods during the summer of 1962. (A. Simpkins)

THE CREW of 'Barnum' class 2–4–0 No. 3213 pose for the photographer at Kennington Junction in the summer of 1912. (Author's Collection)

STORM DAMAGE AT HINKSEY. This view looks south and shows the Redbridge in the distance. The flooded land on the right was infilled during the Second World War to form Hinksey marshalling yards. (Author's Collection)

AN ENLARGEMENT of one of the flood pictures shows the Great Western halt at Hinksey, opened in 1908 and closed in 1915. (Author's Collection)

'QUEEN' CLASS 2–2–2 NO. 1128 hurries past Abingdon Road Halt with a London service in around 1912. The engine, built in 1875, survived at Oxford until its withdrawal in 1914. (Author's Collection)

THE RCTS EAST MIDLANDER RAILTOUR from Nottingham to Swindon, hauled by ex-Midland 4–4–0 No. 40454, passes through Oxford on 6 May 1956. (A.R. Davis)

'COUNTY' CLASS 4–6–0 NO. 1025 *County of Radnor* passes Hinksey South on 2 July 1960 with the 10.20 a.m. service from Weymouth to Wolverhampton. (J.F. Loader)

'WEST COUNTRY' PACIFIC NO. 34043 *Combe Martin* passes the wartime constructed marshalling yard at Hinksey on its approach to Oxford in the summer of 1958. (J.D. Edwards)

'HALL' CLASS 5984 *Linden Hall* approaches Oxford with a service from Paddington passing, on the left, part of the gasworks complex and, on the right, the northern entrance to Hinksey yards. (Courtesy A. Vaughan)

GREAT WESTERN RAILWAY.

OXFORD & CAMBRIDGE BOAT RACE.

On SATURDAY, APRIL 5th, 1884,

A CHEAP EXCURSION.

FOR 1 OR 3 DAYS,

WILL LEAVE	a.m.	WILL LEAVE	a.m.
Wolverhampton (Low Level) ....at	3 15	Warwick .... at	4 24
Bilston .... „	3 22	Leamington .... „	4 33
Wednesbury .... „	3 28	Banbury .... „	5 5
West Bromwich .... „	3 36	Oxford .... „	5 45
Hockley .... „	3 43	Abingdon .... „	5 40
Snow Hill (Birmingham) ...... „	3 50	Reading .... „	6 35
Bordesley .... „	3 54		

FOR

LONDON

Arriving at Paddington at 7.30 a.m.

FARES THERE AND BACK.

	From Wolver-hampton.	From Bilston, Wednes-bury or West Brom-wich.	From Hockley, Birming-ham or Bordesley.	From Warwick or Leaming-ton.	From Banbury.	From Oxford.	From Abing-don.	From Reading.
DAY TRIP, 3rd Class	7/6	7/6	7/-	6/6	6/-	5/-	5/-	4/-
Returning April 7th, 3rd Class...	12/-	11/-	10/-	9/-	8/-	7/-	...	...
Returning April 7th, 1st Class ...	22/-	21/-	20/-	18/-	16/-	14/-	...	...

First Class Day Trip Tickets issued at double the Third Class fares.

CRYSTAL PALACE.—Through Excursion Tickets to the CRYSTAL PALACE, including admission, and available for return from Paddington on April 5th or 7th at times shewn below, will also be issued by above Train, as under:—

2/3 First Class, and 1/6 Third Class in addition to the London Fares.

These Tickets may be used between London and the Crystal Palace on April 5th or 7th. The Tickets by the Brighton Company's route must be used either from Victoria, London Bridge, or Kensington (Addison Road) Stations, and by the London Chatham and Dover Company's route from the Victoria, Holborn Viaduct or Ludgate Hill Stations.

Children under 3 years of Age, Free ; 3 and under 12, Half-price.

RETURN ARRANGEMENTS.

Passengers with Day Trip Tickets return from the PADDINGTON STATION at 7.20 p.m., and Westbourne Park at 7.25 p.m. April 5th ; Reading Passengers can also return from Paddington at 9.20 p.m. ; Passengers holding Tickets at the Higher Fares return on the following Monday, April 7th, from Paddington Station at 6.25 p.m., and Westbourne Park at 6.30 p.m.

The Tickets are not transferable, and are only available by the specified Train. Passengers using them by any other Train will be charged the full Ordinary Fare. One Package of Luggage only allowed, at Passenger's own risk.

Frequent Trains run from and to Kensington, Paddington and Westbourne Park, and all Stations on the Metropolitan and District Railways, including South Kensington, Victoria, Westminster Bridge, Temple, Blackfriars, Mansion House, Aldgate, Bishopsgate, Moorgate Street, Farringdon Street and Baker Street.

Tickets, Bills and every information can be obtained at the Stations. Tickets and Bills can also be obtained at the following G. W. Parcels Receiving Offices in Birmingham :—Mr. Smithson, Easy Row ; Mr. Street, Hen and Chickens, Worcester Street ; Mr. Robinson, Constitution Hill ; Mr. Cashmore, 283, Summer Lane, and Mr. Cowdery, 146, Hockley Hill.

PADDINGTON, *March*, 1884.　　　　　　　J. GRIERSON, *General Manager.*

(35)　　　　Waterlow and Sons Limited, Printers, London Wall, London.

A POSTER advertising a cheap excursion to view the Oxford vs Cambridge boat race on Saturday 5 April 1884. (courtesy D. Castle)

THE OXFORD GAS LIGHT AND COKE COMPANY was founded in 1818 and had established sidings adjacent to the Great Western main line by 1886. In 1926 a new works was constructed to the south of the Thames. Over the years the company owned and operated four small locomotives. The following pictures show them all. The first is William Bagnall 0–4–0ST, works No. 1839. The engine was built for the company in 1906 and survived on the gasworks system until 1949. (J.B. Stoyel)

THE SECOND GASWORKS ENGINE was Peckett and Son No. 1682, pictured here in the old works in 1958. It was purchased new by the company in 1925 and was withdrawn from service when the gasworks closed in 1960. (J.D. Edwards)

WILLIAM BAGNALL 0–4–0ST NO. 2656 was purchased new in 1942 and withdrawn and scrapped on site in 1957. It is pictured at Oxford in 1953. (J.B. Stoyel)

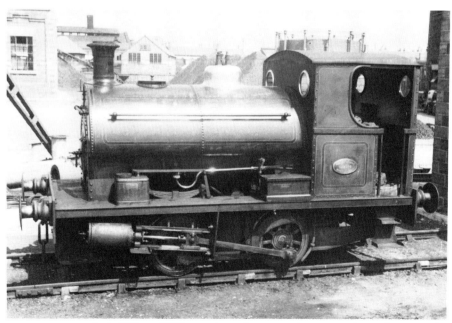

PECKETT AND SONS 0–4–0ST NO. 2075 was always known as the new engine at the gasworks. It was purchased from new by the company in 1946 and withdrawn in 1960. (J.B. Stoyel)

THE PLEASURES OF PUNTING ON THE THAMES are depicted on the cover of this 1950 publicity handout. (Author's Collection)

'DUKE' CLASS 4–4–0 NO. 3256 *Guinevere* passes through Oxford with a 'Down' goods service on 8 June 1933. (Author's Collection)

'COUNTY' CLASS 4–4–0 NO. 3811 *County of Bucks* stands at Oxford station with a service to Princes Risborough, *c.* 1930. (Real Photos)

THIS RARE PHOTOGRAPH shows 'River' class 2–4–0 No. 73 *Isis* in the 'Down' bay at Oxford with a stopping service to Banbury on 21 May 1914. (Author's Collection)

GREAT WESTERN RAILWAY.

IMPORTANT NOTICE!

In consequence of the continuance of the Coal Labour troubles it has been found necessary to further curtail the Passenger Train Services on and from **Friday, March 22nd.**

Trains from Oxford.

Time of Departure.	DOWN TRAINS. Destination.	Time of Departure.	UP TRAINS. Destination.
2. 2 a.m.	Banbury, Leamington, Birmingham, and the North. (Mondays excepted.)	2.50 a.m.	To Swindon, Bath and Bristol. (Mondays excepted).
7.50 „	Stopping Train to Birmingham.	7. 5 „	To Radley, Culham and Didcot. Connects to Swindon, Newbury, Winchester and Reading.
8. 5 „	Stopping Train to Moreton-in-Marsh, Evesham, Worcester and Wolverhampton.	7.10 „	Paddington via Thame.
8.42 „	Banbury, Leamington, Birmingham and Wolverhampton.	8.26 „	Paddington via Thame.
		8.45 „	Radley, Culham, Didcot, Reading and Paddington.
9. 0 „	To Banbury and Great Central Line.	9.12 „	Reading and Paddington.
9.20 „	To Witney and Fairford.	9.35 „	Radley, Culham, Didcot. Connects to Swindon and the West.
11.20 „	To Banbury, Leamington, Birmingham, Wolverhampton, Shrewsbury, Dolgelley, Barmouth, and Cambrian Line, Chester and Birkenhead.	11. 0 „	To Reading and Paddington.
		11.20 „	Paddington via Thame.
11.25 „	Stopping Train to Evesham and Worcester.	11.35 „	All Stations to Didcot and Reading.
		1. 0 p.m.	Reading and Paddington.
11.35 „	Stopping Train to Banbury.	1. 6 „	All Stations to Didcot and Reading.
3. 8 p.m.	Stopping Train to Evesham and Worcester.	1.54 „	Reading and Paddington.
		2.28 „	Paddington via Thame.
3.52 „	Banbury, Leamington, Birmingham and Wolverhampton.	2.48 „	All Stations to Didcot, also to Newbury, Winchester, Swindon and Reading.
4.25 „	To Witney and Fairford.	4.25 „	Didcot and Paddington, also all Stations Didcot to Reading.
6, 9 „	Banbury, Leamington, Warwick, Birmingham, Wolverhampton, Shrewsbury, Chester and Birkenhead.	4.58 „	All Stations to Didcot.
		5.50 „	Reading and Paddington.
6.15 „	Principal Stations to Evesham, Worcester and Wolverhampton.	5.57 „	Stations to Didcot, Reading and Swindon.
		6.25 „	Paddington via Thame.
6.30 „	Stopping Train to Birmingham.	7.40 „	Didcot, Newbury and Winchester, and Stations to Swindon.
8.40 „	To Witney and Fairford.		
8.49 „	Banbury, Leamington and Principal Stations to Birmingham, Wolverhampton and Shrewsbury.	8.45 „	Stations to Didcot.
		9.29 „	Reading and Paddington.
8.55 „	Principal Stations to Evesham and Worcester.	9.40 „	Stations to Didcot, Swindon, South Wales, West of England, also connects to Reading and Paddington.
10. 0 „	To Banbury and Great Central Line. (Saturdays excepted).		

BY ORDER.

PADDINGTON, *March*, 1912.

WYMAN & SONS, Printers, London and Reading.

50

PART OF THE 'DOWN' PLATFORM AT OXFORD on 7 September 1967. The condition of the platform at this point defies description. (Author's Collection)

Left:
THE MINERS' STRIKE in 1912 caused the Great Western many problems which resulted in a number of services being cancelled due to coal shortages. This notice, dated 22 March 1912, informed the Oxford public of the cancellation of a further forty-three services. (Author's Collection)

THIS VIEW OF THE 'DOWN' PLATFORM AT OXFORD was taken on 17 October 1935. (Author's Collection)

EX-GREAT WESTERN MOGUL 2–6–0 NO. 5330 draws the attention of a group of train spotters as it passes through Oxford on 10 August 1955 with a holiday extra. (Author's Collection)

COLLEGES AT OXFORD, ROAD DRIVE TO ABINGDON & STEAMER CRUISE
ON THE
Glorious River Thames

EACH MONDAY

May 23rd to September 19th, inclusive (except Mondays, June 6th and August 1st). Also Tuesdays, June 7th and August 2nd.

Half-Day Excursions to OXFORD

Including a CONDUCTED TOUR OF THE COLLEGES, ROAD DRIVE TO ABINGDON, TEA. STEAMER TRIP from ABINGDON TO OXFORD.

Forward	PADDINGTON	..	depart	11 15 a.m.
	OXFORD ..	..	arrive	12 38 p.m.
Return	OXFORD ..	..	depart	7 53 p.m.
	PADDINGTON	..	arrive	9 20 p.m.

ITINERARY.

RAIL ..	..	To Oxford (arrive 12.38 p.m.) Interval for Luncheon.
TOUR ..	..	At 2.0 p.m. join special bus at Bus Station, Gloucester Green, for CONDUCTED TOUR OF THE COLLEGES in charge of Official Guides, visiting as far as possible, Worcester College, Martyrs' Memorial, Trinity and New Colleges, Radcliffe Square, etc.
DRIVE..	..	At the conclusion of tour passengers remain in Buses for DRIVE TO ABINGDON, passing through Bagley Woods, arriving 4.15 p.m.
TEA ..	..	Served in Abingdon and is included in the charge.
STEAMER	,,	From Abingdon Bridge at 5.15 p.m., passing Nuneham Park, Radley, Sandford, Kennington, Iffley, the Oxford University Race Course and the College Barges, arriving Oxford 7.0 p.m.
RAIL ..	..	From OXFORD at 7.53 p.m.

INCLUSIVE FARES.

FIRST CLASS ..	..	13/-	Adults	9/3 Children (under 14 years of age)
THIRD CLASS ..	..	10/6	,,	8/- ,, ,, ,,

(Fares cover Rail Fare, Tour of Colleges, Road Drive, Tea and Steamer Cruise).

NOTICE AS TO CONDITIONS.—These Tickets are issued subject to the Notices and Conditions shewn in the current Time Tables. For LUGGAGE ALLOWANCES also see Time Tables.

Any further information may be obtained from Mr. C. T. Cox, Divisional Superintendent, Paddington, or from Mr. F. R. POTTER, Superintendent of the Line, Paddington Station, W.2. (Telephone : Paddington 7000, Extn. " Enquiries " ; 8.0 a.m. to 10.0 p.m.)

PADDINGTON, March, 1938.   JAMES MILNE, General Manager.

Printed in Great Britain by WYMAN & SONS LTD., London, Reading and Fakenham.—10162.
L.D. 173.   10,000 D.S.   A.D. 10,000.   5,000 G.E.B.   T4/95446.

THE GREAT WESTERN ran regular trips to Oxford which also included a trip on the Thames, as seen on the above poster dated March 1938. (Author's Collection)

DUKEDOG 4–4–0 NO. 9023 passes Walton Well, Oxford with a goods service from Hinksey Yard to Fairford on 28 July 1951. (R. Bowen)

THE INTERIOR of the signal box at Oxford Station North in the early 1950s. (Author's Collection)

THE 'DOWN' SIDE TICKET OFFICE AT OXFORD in 1962. Ticket clerk David Green is on the right; the other is unidentified. (Author's Collection)

EX-GREAT EASTERN B12 4–6–0 NO. 61546 prepares to depart from the 'Down' bay at Oxford with the 2.28 p.m. service to Bletchley, Bedford and Cambridge in April 1959. (J.D. Edwards)

EX-GREAT WESTERN DIESEL RAILCAR NO. 16 stands in the 'Up' middle road at Oxford on 8 June 1957. (Author's Collection)

THIS EARLIER PICTURE, taken in around 1947, shows car No. 11 leaving the 'Down' bay at Oxford with a service to Woodstock. (Oxfordshire County Libraries)

A THROUGH SERVICE from York to Bournemouth, hauled by rebuilt 'West Country' class 34028 *Eddystone*, passes over the Botley Road bridge as it departs from Oxford in June 1961. (W. Turner)

A WONDERFUL PICTURE FOR BUS FANS. A corner of the old bus station at Gloucester Green taken in 1958. The whole area has now been redeveloped; even The Greyhound pub is but a memory. (J.D. Edwards)

AN AEC 'BRIDGEMASTER' BUS just passes under the 13 ft 6 in clearance of the Botley Road railway bridge in around 1958. (J.D. Edwards)

THE RESULT of a normal height double deck bus passing under the restricted height of the station bridge. (R.H. Simpson)

GAS TURBINE NO. 18000 stands at Oxford on 24 April 1950. It had worked in on a special test train prior to being officially accepted by the Western Region. (R.H.G. Simpson)

A GROUP OF NAVVIES pose for the camera at Cassington during construction of the Eynsham section of the Oxford Northern bypass in around 1933. On the right can be seen one of the small Kerr Stuart 0–4–0 locomotives hired by Oxfordshire County Council from Aubrey Watson Ltd to assist with spoil removal. (Packer Collection)

KERR STUART No. 4292 at Wolvercote in July 1933. (B.D. Stoyel)

A TRAINLOAD OF PREFABRICATED BRIDGE GIRDERS for the construction of the new A40 road bridge at Wolvercote stands at Oxford North in 1934. On the right can be seen Oxford North Signal Box, removed during 1940 and replaced by a new box when the new junction at Oxford was opened. (Courtesy J. Peverall Cooper)

WOLVERCOTE JUNCTION shortly after work had started on the new roadbridge over the railway. (Courtesy J. Peverall Cooper)

THE BRIDGE BEGINS TO TAKE SHAPE. (Courtesy J. Peverall Cooper)

A GROUP OF RAILWAY ENTHUSIASTS FROM OXFORD getting very wet while on a visit to Derby locomotive works in 1971. Some of those identified are Sheard, Garrod, Bowen, Wilkinson, Welch and the author. (R. McAvoy)

WESTERN REGION LOCO-FIREMAN JOHN CHURCH pauses for the cameraman shortly before leaving home for his next turn of duty at Oxford. (Courtesy John Church)

THE TRACK LAYOUT PANEL at Oxford Station North Box. (B. Higgins)

THE NORTH END OF OXFORD STATION has changed somewhat since 1960, almost every structure on the picture having either been removed or altered. Even the tower of St Barnabas' church has since been rebuilt. (Author's Collection)

'BRITANNIA' PACIFIC NO. 70002 *Geoffrey Chaucer* accelerates away through Oxford with the Morris Cowley to Bathgate service in 1962. (S. Boorne)

EX-LMS 2–6–0T NO. 42106 stands in the 'Up' bay at Oxford with the 9.35 a.m. service from Bletchley in May 1960. (Author's Collection)

GREAT WESTERN RAILWAY.
BIRMINGHAM CATTLE & DOG SHOW.
On Thursday, November 30th, 1882,
A
CHEAP EXCURSION TRAIN
FOR
BIRMINGHAM

WILL LEAVE						A.M.	Fares There & Back. Third Class.
Oxford ...	...	...	...	...	at	7 15	**5s. 0d.**
Handborough ...	...	...	...	,,		7 35	**4s. 0d.**
Charlbury ...	...	...	...	,,		7 45	
Shipton ...	...	...	...	,,		8 0	
Chipping Norton Junction	...	...	,,			8 10	**3s. 6d.**
Chipping Norton	...	...	,,			7 50	
Addlestrop ...	...	...	...	,,		8 15	
Moreton-in-Marsh ...	...	...	,,			8 30	
Blockley ...	...	...	...	,,		8 35	**3s. 0d.**
Campden ...	...	...	...	,,		8 45	
Honeybourne ...	...	...	...	,,		9 10	
Pershore ...	...	...	...	,,		8 20	
Fladbury ...	...	...	...	,,		8 30	**2s. 6d.**
Evesham ...	...	...	...	,,		8 35	
Long Marston ...	...	...	...	,,		9 20	
Milcote ...	...	...	...	,,		9 30	
Stratford-on-Avon ...	...	...	,,			9 40	
Bearley ...	...	...	...	,,		9 50	**2s. 0d.**
Alcester ...	...	...	...	,,		9 40	
Great Alne ...	...	...	...	,,		9 45	
Hatton ...	...	...	...	,,		10 15	**1s. 6d.**

First Class Tickets issued at Double above Fares.

Children under 3 Years of Age, Free ; 3 and under 12, Half-price.
Passengers are allowed One Package of Personal Luggage Free, but it must be distinctly understood that it is conveyed entirely at their own risk.
The Tickets are not Transferable, and only available by the Excursion Train; if used by any other Train the full Ordinary Fare will be charged.

The **RETURN TRAIN** will leave BIRMINGHAM, Snow Hill Station, the same day, as under :—
For Great Alne and Alcester at 6.0 p.m.
For all other places ... ... at 8.5 p.m.

PADDINGTON, *November*, 1882.　　　　J. GRIERSON, *General Manager*.

Waterlow and Sons Limited, Printers, London Wall, London.

STEAM AT NIGHT – what a wonderful sight. No. 4956 *Plowden Hall* at Oxford with the 'Up' Grimsby to Swindon fish service. (J.D. Edwards)

Left:
A POSTER advertising a trip to the Birmingham Cattle and Dog Show. Note that the train ran via Honeybourne and Stratford-upon-Avon. (Author's Collection)

THE INTERIOR of Oxford Station North Box during its last night of operation on 12 October 1973. (B. Higgins)

THE UPPER QUADRANT SIGNALS at Oxford North Junction on 24 January 1951. These experimental signals were manufactured at the Caversham Road signal works in Reading. They survived in use at Oxford until 1973. Today they are preserved in the National Railway Museum at York. (Author's Collection)

EX GREAT WESTERN 2 8 0 NO. 3820 moves slowly through Oxford with an oil train from Fawley, Southampton to Bromford Bridge on 16 November 1963. (D. Tuck)

EX-GREAT WESTERN DIESEL RAILCAR No. 23, painted in BR Green, stands at the 'Down' bay platform at Oxford with a service to Worcester in 1962. (J. Turner)

THE REMAINS OF THE 1972 'TEMPORARY' STATION AT OXFORD shortly before its demolition in 1989. (Author's Collection)

EX-LNWR WEBB 0–6–0 NO. 8432 takes water at Oxford Rewley Road engine shed, c. 1931. (Courtesy D. Holmes)

A GROUP OF LOCAL RAILWAY ENTHUSIASTS pictured at Oxford on 3 July 1932. They are, left to right: M. Butterfield, M. Castle, B. Holmes, R. Savage, G. Wheeler, E. Arthurs, R. Bassington, B. Baulk, J. Symes, L. Jarvis. (Author's Collection)

EX-LNWR WEBB 0–6–0T NO. 7733 poses for the photographer on the swing bridge at Oxford Rewley Road in June 1930. (Author's Collection)

EX-LANCASHIRE AND YORKSHIRE 3F 0–6–0 NO. 12086 stands at Rewley Road in around 1946.
(G. Hine)

A POSTCARD publicizing the Micheline railcar. (Author's Collection)

THE MICHELINE EXPERIMENTAL RAILCAR is seen here crossing the swing bridge over the Sheepwash Channel *en route* to Oxford Rewley Road in April 1932. (Courtesy D. Holmes)

THE INTERIOR of the ex-LNWR station at Oxford Rewley Road. (Author's Collection)

EX-LNWR BOWEN-COOKE 0–8–0 NO. 9350 stands alongside the ex-LNWR shed at Rewley Road, Oxford, C. 1930. (Author's Collection)

FOWLER 4F 0–6–0 NO. 4398 stands at Rewley Road in June 1932. (Courtesy D. Holmes)

THE EX-LONDON AND NORTH WESTERN STATION at Oxford Rewley Road pictured on 6 December 1935. On the right stands the station master's house. Notice also the offices of Wagon Repairs Limited in the centre. (Author's Collection)

THE FRONT OF THE EX-LNWR STATION at Rewley Road possibly taken just after the Second World War. Although the station is long closed to passengers the coffee hut in the foreground is still open. (Author's Collection)

THIS VIEW OF THE ENTRANCE TO REWLEY ROAD STATION in around 1930 also shows to good effect Frank Cooper's Marmalade factory, now an antiques centre. (Author's Collection)

LNWR WEBB 0–6–0 SADDLE TANK NO. 3185 stands alongside the Thames at Oxford Rewley Road engine shed sometime prior to the Second World War. (Author's Collection)

EX-LNWR 4–4–0 NO. 3177 *Merlin* stands at Oxford Rewley Road loco yard in around 1930. (Author's Collection)

EX-MIDLAND RAILWAY 3P NO. 40743 at Aristotle Lane, Oxford with a goods service in March 1952. (J.B. Snell)

A PETROL TRAIN to Yarnton, hauled by Eastern Region 0–6–0 No. 64688, passes the grain sidings at Oxford Road Junction, Kidlington in around 1953. (Author's Collection)

REWLEY ROAD STATION: AN ELEGY

Rewley Road Station has been closed,
The L.M.S. as we used to call it
In the good old days before nationalisation,
Or the London and North-Western
In the still better and older days
Before amalgamation,
When the carriages were painted white
And the engines blue:
No, that was the Caledonian,
Its opposite number across the Border;
But at least it was different, different,
And now everything is the same, the same, the same.
How sweet was the old L.M.S. Station,
How quiet, how calm,
With almost no one on the platform
And few in the train,
Just an old porter or two
Willing to serve you:
It was dearer to us than the Great Western
And nearer by the odd threepence in the taxi;
And you could call your soul your own.
It was a terminus, either alpha or omega.
From there the train began:
There it ended:
It was complete and final:
It filled you with restfulness.
How many generations of young men
Have come down from Scotland,
From Lancashire and the north,
From Ireland via Stranraer or Heysham or Liverpool
    or Holyhead,
Seeking the way to Oxford,
Finding their goal at Oxford,
Their aspirations, ambitions and dreams.
Changing at Bletchley, patiently, quietly,
Disregarding the surface ugliness,
Because Bletchley is good and great,
It is a door, an avenue
To Oxford and to Cambridge,
To all who seek the life of learning,
Janua Vitae.
You climb into the little train:
It puffs bravely off:
Swanbourne, Winslow, Verney Junction,
Marsh Gibbon, Launton, Claydon, Bicester;
Then from Islip it gathers speed
On its last and longest stretch,
Faster and faster,
Rattling along past Godstow,
Past Port Meadow,

And you saw the first sight of Oxford,
Oxford, Oxford, Oxford.
The dreaming spires,
Actually it was only the Campanile of St. Barnabas,
But it stood for all the rest,
And then the train slowed down,
Rattled to a stop
And you got out on the quiet platform
And gathered your luggage
And drove nervously, diffidently, excitedly
To the College which had accepted you.
But now it is all over:
You may still come by Bletchley,
By Marsh Gibbon and by Islip,
But you will end up in a rotten little bay
In the Great Western Station,
Or Western Region as they call it now,
With the snobs from London,
The cads from Birmingham,
The bumpkins from the West Country
And the assertive and garrulous Welsh.
It is all over now:
Eheu fugaces, Postume, Postume;
Ichabod, Ichabod, the glory is departed:
But I will not have it:
I will not bow to the yoke.
Non ego, as Virgil has expressed it,
Myrmidonum sedes, it comes, I think, from the Second
    Aeneid,
Dolopumve superbas, aspiciam.
Rather than be shunted into the Great Western,
I will travel, as a matter of principle,
To Oxford
By road.

VERNON FORK.

THE CLOSURE OF REWLEY ROAD to passenger traffic in 1951 prompted a Mr Vernon Fork to write the above lament which was duly published in the October 1951 edition of the *Oxford Magazine*. (Courtesy Oxonian Press)

FORMER GREAT EASTERN D16 4–4–0 NO. 62571 backs out of Rewley Road after bringing in the 12.18 p.m. service from Cambridge on 28 September 1951, the last week of passenger services into this station. (Dr G.D. Parks)

BR STANDARD CLASS 4 NO. 75052 passes the wartime constructed sidings at Port Meadow with a service to Bletchley. (J.D. Edwards)

BR STANDARD CLASS 4 NO. 75038 passes Oxford Port Meadow Box with a service from Bletchley. The box and siding in the foreground were opened on 14 December 1941 and closed on 9 June 1958. (B. Higgins)

THE REPLACEMENT SIGNAL BOX at Oxford Banbury Road Junction on 23 January 1959. The old box stood just to the left of the new one. (British Railways)

THE EXTERIOR of the closed ex-LNWR station at Rewley Road, Oxford in 1958. (J.D. Edwards)

MEMBERS OF THE GREAT WESTERN SOCIETY stand alongside army 0–6–0 No. 197 *Sapper* at Bicester Ordnance depot on the occasion of an official visit in 1973. (D. Turner)

A BR CLASS 08 SHUNTER NO. 08803 'off the rails' in the now closed Rewley Road yard on 17 June 1975. The pile of stone is from the adjacent Axtell and Perry stonemason's yard, now also gone. (D. Parker)

PROBABLY THE MOST FAMOUS of all of the 517 class of engines was No. 1473 *Fair Rosamund.* The only named member of the class, it was associated with the Woodstock Branch for almost the whole of its working life. It is seen here at Oxford on Whit Sunday 5 June 1927. (Great Western Trust)

DIMINUTIVE EX-ALEXANDRA DOCKS 0–4–0ST NO. 1341 stands outside the works at Oxford on 22 April 1930. The engine had apparently suffered a hot box while passing through Oxford. (Author's Collection)

LNER 4–6–0 NO. 2865 *Leicester City* stands outside the engine shed at Oxford on 11 April 1937 having worked in from Leicester with a cross country service. The engine is named after the football team, not the city. (Author's Collection)

EX-GWR 2181 CLASS 0–6–0 NO. 2182, newly outshopped from Wolverhampton Works, stands in the yard at Oxford in the early 1950s. (Author's Collection)

EX-SWINDON WORKS 2–6–2T NO. 5227 stands dead at Oxford on 12 February 1960. It had failed with a hot box while working through on a running in turn. (Author's Collection)

THE INTERIOR of the small lifting shop at Oxford MPD. (R.H.G. Simpson)

EX-GWR DIESEL RAILCAR NO. 15 stands at Oxford Loco in 1951. At Oxford these vehicles were generally used on services to Princes Risborough. (Author's Collection)

850 CLASS 0–6–0PT NO. 1935 stands alongside the small works at Oxford in the early 1950s. The engine was allocated to Oxford from 1937 until its withdrawal in 1953. (G, Hine)

FRANCO-CROSTI 9F NO. 92027 stands at Attwoods siding, Oxford, c. 1958. (John Hubbard)

NO. 7412, sporting what appears to be an oil drum extension to the chimney, stands in store at Oxford in 1962. (W. Turner)

'MERCHANT NAVY' CLASS NO. 35023 *Holland-Afrika Line* on the turntable at Oxford in 1963. (D. Tuck)

HIGH SUMMER AT OXFORD SHED! Ex-LMS 8F No. 48120 appears to be almost overwhelmed with vegetation as it awaits its next turn of duty in June 1961. (W. Turner)

EX-GREAT EASTERN CLASS J20 0–6–0 No. 64688 takes a well earned rest at Oxford, having worked in from Cambridge, c. 1956. (Author's Collection)

'BRITANNIA' PACIFIC NO. 70054 *Dornoch Firth* stands in the sun at Oxford in almost ex-works condition on 9 June 1963. (D. Tuck)

BR STANDARD 9F 2–10–0 NO. 92224 at Oxford in 1961. (W. Turner)

AN UNUSUAL VISITOR TO OXFORD is ex-LMS 'Patriot' No. 45523 *Bangor*. It stands in the yard at Oxford Shed in 1963 having worked in to the city with a goods service from the Bletchley line. (D. Tuck)

LOOKING RATHER THE WORSE FOR WEAR is 'Battle of Britain' class 4–6–2 No. 34061 *73 Squadron* receiving attention at Oxford in July 1963. (D. Tuck)

'KING ARTHUR' CLASS 4–6–0 NO. 30763 *Sir Bors De Ganis* stands on the turntable road at Oxford. The engine has been turned, coaled and watered in preparation for working back to Bournemouth. (J.D. Edwards)

OXFORD ENGINE SHED YARD in June 1961 with a line of redundant steam locomotives (three 'Halls' and two 'Castles'), all withdrawn and awaiting the torch. (W. Turner)

THE END OF STEAM TRACTION AT OXFORD came with the closing of the steam locomotive depot on 3 January 1966. This sad picture was taken shortly after then and shows the rows of redundant steam engines awaiting their final trip to the scrap yard. (Author's Collection)

WOLVERCOTE SIDING SIGNAL BOX pictured shortly before its closure. The box, which was opened in 1900, was closed on 9 June 1958. (J.D. Edwards)

0–6–0 NO. 2221 crosses the junction at Wolvercote with a Fairford to Oxford service in around 1959. (J.D. Edwards)

NO. 7013 *BRISTOL CASTLE* leaves the Worcester line at Wolvercote Junction with the 'Up' 'Cathedrals Express' on a cloudless summer day. (Dr G. Smith)

'CASTLE' CLASS 4–6–0 NO. 7004 *Eastnor Castle* storms through Combe Halt in July 1961 with a service from Paddington to Worcester. (Revd R.T. Jones)

SECTION THREE

The Branch Lines

THE FRONTAGE OF HENLEY STATION c. 1900. Note the horse-drawn cabs awaiting passengers. (Author's Collection)

THE WANTAGE TRAMWAY CO. HUGHES TRAM ENGINE NO. 3 together with cars 1 and 4 near Wantage Road station, c. 1905. (F. Burgess)

TRAM ENGINE NO. 6 and two of the four wheeled cars stand redundant at Wantage, c. 1930. (LGRP)

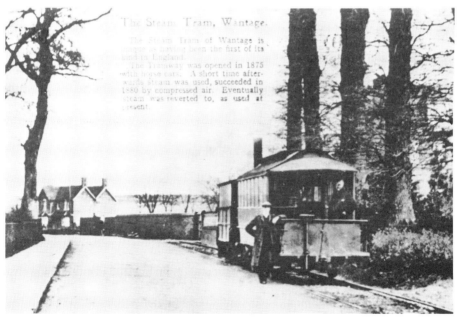

WANTAGE TRAMWAY HUGHES TRAM ENGINE AND CAR NO. 3 pictured near Wantage around the turn of the century. (Author's Collection)

517 CLASS 0–4–2T NO. 1484 leaves Cholsey with the 2.05 p.m. service to Wallingford on 22 April 1924. (LCGB/Ken Nunn Collection)

THE WALLINGFORD BRANCH SERVICE prepares to leave Cholsey and Moulsford on 18 April 1959. (A. McDougall)

THIS POSTCARD VIEW shows the entrance to Wallingford station in around 1909. (Author's Collection)

A SERVICE TO CHOLSEY, hauled by 517 class 0–4–2T No. 1479, awaits departure from Wallingford on 1 November 1930. (Author's Collection)

WALLINGFORD STATION shortly after closure in 1959. (Author's Collection)

0–4–2T NO. 1466 TOGETHER WITH AUTO-COACH 231 are seen here near Cholsey on 15 April 1968. The preserved engine and coach were working a special service over the Wallingford Branch in connection with the Wallingford carnival. (Great Western Society)

THIS VIEW OF THE DESERTED TERMINUS AT WATLINGTON was taken in 1957, just a few months before closure. (J.D. Edwards)

THE FOLLOWING PICTURES show some of the low level halts on the Watlington Branch. All were closed when services to Watlington were withdrawn on 1 July 1957. This is Wainhill Crossing.

KINGSTON CROSSING.

0–6–0T NO. 1636 ON SHUNTING DUTY at Chinnor in around 1959. (J.D. Edwards)

LEWKNOR BRIDGE.

BLEDLOW BRIDGE, included for completeness although situated in Buckinghamshire. (J. Edwards)

GREAT WESTERN STEAM RAILMOTOR NO. 54 pauses at Abingdon Road halt with an Oxford to Princes Risborough service in June 1914. (Author's Collection)

FARES. (3rd Class.)

FROM	Oxford. s. d.	Hinksey Halt. s. d.	Abingdon Road Halt. s. d.	Iffley Halt. s. d.	Littlemore. s. d.	Garsington Bridge Halt. s. d.	Horsepath Halt. s. d.	Wheatley. s. d.	Tiddington. d.	Thame. d.	Bledlow. d.
Hinksey Halt	1½	—									
Abingdon Road Halt	2	1	—								
Iffley Halt	2½	1½	1	—							
Littlemore	3	2	1½	1	—						
Garsington Bridge Halt	5	3½	3	2½	1½	—					
Horsepath Halt	6	5	4½	3½	3	1½	—				
Wheatley	8	6½	6	5	4½	3	1½	—			
Tiddington	11	10	9½	8½	8	6½	5	3½	—		
Thame	1 3½	1 2	1 1½	1 0½	1 0	10½	9	7½	4	—	
Bledlow	1 7½	1 6	1 5½	1 5	1 4	1 2½	1 1	11½	8	4	—
Princes Risborough	1 9	1 8	1 7	1 6½	1 5½	1 4	1 3	1 1	10	5½	1½

FROM	Oxford. s. d.	Wolvercot Halt. d.	Kidlington. d.	Blenheim & Woodstock. d.	Bletchington. d.
Wolvercot Halt	2	—			
Kidlington	5½	3½	—		
Blenheim & Woodstock	9	7	3½	—	
Bletchington	7½	5½	2	6	—
Heyford	1 0	9½	6	10	4

FROM	Oxford. s. d.	Yarnton. s. d.	Handborough. d.	Charlbury. d.	Ascott-under-Wychwood. d.
Yarnton	4	—			
Handborough	7	3	—		
Charlbury	1 1	9½	6	—	
Ascott-under-Wychwood	1 5	1 1	10	3½	—
Shipton	1 6	1 2½	11	5	1½

RAILMOTOR FARES c. 1909.

LITTLEMORE STATION in the mid-1950s. (Author's Collection)

A VIEW OF MORRIS COWLEY STATION, c. 1930. Although the station is long gone, Morris Cowley is today the main freight centre for the Oxford area. (LGRP)

A SLIGHT CONFRONTATION at Morris Cowley between ex-LMS 8F No. 48134 on the Washwood Heath to Morris Cowley service and 'Hall' class 4–6–0 No. 6979 *Helperly Hall* on the West London parcels on 12 January 1961. Both engines were subsequently repaired. (Author's Collection)

CLASS 47 DIESEL ELECTRIC NO. D1741 approaches Horspath Tunnel with a diverted Wolverhampton to Paddington service on 19 March 1967. (S. Boorne)

HORSPATH HALT stood midway between Morris Cowley and Wheatley. It was opened in June 1933 and closed in January 1963. (Author's Collection)

THIS PACKER VIEW OF WHEATLEY VILLAGE AND STATION was taken from the adjacent wood yard of Messrs Avery's sawmill in the 1920s. (Packer Collection)

EX-GREAT WESTERN 4–4–0 NO. 9017 on an enthusiasts' special crosses the bridge over the Cuddesdon Road at Wheatley on 20 April 1958. (H.W. Burchell)

THE NEAT AND TIDY STATION AT TIDDINGTON on a summer day in 1961. (Author's Collection)

NO. 6129 STANDS AT THAME with a service to Princes Risborough in April 1961. The oil terminal that has sustained this section of line since it was closed to passenger traffic in 1963 has itself now closed, leaving the future of the section in doubt. (Photomatic)

THE DELIGHTFUL OVERALL ROOF of Thame station can be seen in this view taken in around 1959. (Author's Collection)

FEW PASSENGERS AT TOWERSEY. (Author's Collection)

THE ORIGINAL STATION AT ABINGDON around the turn of the century. This building was demolished by a goods train in 1908. (Author's Collection)

A GROUP OF STATION STAFF pose at Abingdon in around 1899. The engine is 850 class saddle tank No. 2017 which was allocated at this time to Didcot shed. (Courtesy D. Castle)

ABINGDON STATION around 1905, with 517 class 0–4–2T No. 1484 waiting to leave with a service to Radley. (Author's Collection)

ABINGDON STATION spruced up and ready for a visit by HM the Queen on 2 November 1956. Note the red carpet along the footpath. (Great Western Trust)

A GENERAL VIEW OF THE TERMINUS AT ABINGDON. (Photomatic)

THE STATION ENTRANCE AT ABINGDON in 1970, just one year before it was demolished. (Author's Collection)

MEMBERS OF THE STATION STAFF together with the crew of 517 class No. 1154 at Radley on 29 April 1912. (Author's Collection)

517 CLASS 0–4–2T NO. 220 stands in the yard at Radley on 17 February 1912 with a goods service for Abingdon. (Author's Collection)

THE ENGINE *FAIR ROSAMUND* NO. 1473, with original open type cab, stands alongside the signal box at Blenheim and Woodstock, c. 1905. (Oxfordshire County Libraries)

THE INTERESTING STATION SIGN AT WOODSTOCK. (Photomatic)

THE EXTERIOR OF WOODSTOCK STATION pictured shortly after closure. (Author's Collection)

WOODSTOCK STATION in 1958, some four years after closure. The building is now in use as a garage, which at the date of this picture was situated across the road from the station. (J.D. Edwards)

PASSENGERS WAIT PATIENTLY as ex-Great Western 0–6–0 No. 5413 arrives at Shipton-on-Cherwell Halt with the service to Woodstock on 20 February 1954. (J. Palmer)

THE 4.10 P.M. SERVICE from Kidlington to Woodstock leaves Shipton-on-Cherwell Halt on 27 February 1954. (Dr G.D. Parkes)

A GROUP OF ENTHUSIASTS waits patiently for a train at Shipton-on-Cherwell Halt. The picture is undated but was possibly taken in February 1954, shortly before the line closed. (Author's Collection)

SHIPTON-ON-CHERWELL HALT was situated adjacent to the A423 road between Oxford and Banbury, the line crossing the road at this point. The entrance to the halt can be seen to the right. (Oxfordshire County Libraries)

THE REMAINS OF SHIPTON-ON-CHERWELL HALT in 1959. (J.D. Edwards)

NO. 1473 *FAIR ROSAMUND* WAITS IN THE BAY at Kidlington with the service to Woodstock, c. 1934. (Author's Collection)

0–4–2T NO. 1420 TOGETHER WITH AUTO-COACH W187W stand in the 'Down' bay at Kidlington on Saturday 27 February 1954, the last day of passenger services between Kidlington and Woodstock. (R. Bowen)

CASSINGTON HALT in the late 1950s. (Author's Collection)

A 'DOWN' SERVICE from Oxford to Fairford, hauled by 0–6–0T No. 7445, stands at Eynsham in around 1959. The 'Down' platform is now to be found at Didcot Railway Centre. (Author's Collection)

THE CONSTRUCTION of the new passing loop and platform at Eynsham on 12 May 1944. (British Railways)

THIS VIEW OF EYNSHAM shows the 'Up' platform in around 1958. (Author's Collection)

NO. 3677 SHUNTS THE OLD YARD AT WITNEY on 13 December 1965. This was the site of the original station at Witney which was opened in 1861 and closed to passenger traffic in 1873 when a new station was opened on the Fairford extension. (M. Yardley)

EX-GREAT WESTERN 0–6–0 NO. 2236 arrives at Witney with a service from Oxford to Fairford on 25 April 1951. The line to the old station at Witney can just be seen behind the signal box. (Author's Collection)

PANNIER TANK NO. 9654 takes water at Witney after arriving with the 12.44 p.m. service from Oxford on 16 June 1962. (M.R. Smith)

THE 'UP' PLATFORM AT BRIZE NORTON c. 1960. (Author's Collection)

LECHLADE STATION was situated just over the border in Gloucestershire. On a cold January day in 1959 0–6–0 No. 2221 waits at the platform with the afternoon pick up goods from Fairford to Oxford. (J.D. Edwards)

A VIEW OF FAIRFORD IN GLOUCESTERSHIRE, just to complete the picture. (Real Photos)

2–6–2T NO. 5514 waits at Chipping Norton with the return service to Kingham in the summer of 1959. (J.D. Edwards)

2–6–2T NO. 5514 AT CHIPPING NORTON in the summer of 1959. The engine has just worked in on a service from Kingham and is seen running round its train in order to form the return working. (J.D. Edwards)

A VIEW OF HOOK NORTON STATION in around 1920. The avoiding lines to the right of the station served a local ironstone quarry. (Packer Collection)

A 517 CLASS 0–4–2T stands at Hook Norton in around 1920 with the auto-train service from Kingham and Chipping Norton to Banbury. (Packer Collection)

BLOXHAM STATION in around 1920. How clean and tidy these country stations looked. Notice also the coal wagon supplying the adjacent Palmer and Sons coal depot. (Packer Collection)

THIS LOVELY PICTURE shows ex-Great Western 0–6–0T No. 5404 at Adderbury with a Banbury to Chipping Norton service. (R.H.G. Simpson)

SECTION FOUR

Oxford to Banbury

THE STATION GARDEN, with unusual flower-pot stands, at Kidlington, c. 1930. (British Railways)

KIDLINGTON STATION, c. 1930. (Author's Collection)

WILLIAM BAGNALL WORKS NO. 2178, built in 1921, stands at Shipton-on-Cherwell cement works in July 1968. The engine, as can be seen, was numbered 2 in the cement works fleet. Withdrawn in 1971, it is preserved on the Yorkshire Dales Railway at Embsay. (D. Parker)

PECKETT 0–6–0 NO. 1378 of 1914, No. 5 *Westminster* in the Blue Circle fleet, stands out of use at Shipton-on-Cherwell cement works in July 1968. (D. Parker)

THE REPLACEMENT MOTIVE POWER AT SHIPTON was a Rolls-Royce Sentinel, works No. 10266, seen here at the cement works in 1968. (D. Parker)

THE 'UP' SIDE PLATFORM AT BLETCHINGTON complete with porter's bicycle is shown to good effect in this 1958 shot. Under the centre arch of the bridge can be seen the large cement works at Shipton-on-Cherwell, now also closed. (J.D. Edwards)

TACKLEY HALT in around 1950. (Author's Collection)

HEYFORD STATION around the turn of the century. The station building on the 'Down' platform (right) is now at Didcot Railway Centre. (Author's Collection)

THIS VIEW OF HEYFORD shows the signal box on the 'Down' platform. (Author's Collection)

OXFORD AND HEYFORD.

WEEK DAYS.

			MK		MT	T		M	M			M	M		
		a.m.	a.m.		a.m.	a.m.	a.m.	p.m.	p.m.		p.m.	p.m.	p.m.	p.m.	p.m.
OXFORD . . . . dep	7 50	8 12	...	9 4	10 35	11 35	12 17	1 57	...	3 25	4 2	5 35	6 30	9 20
Wolvercot Halt . . . . "		8 18		9 50			12 23	2 3	...		4 10	5 41	.	.
Kidlington . . . . "	8 5	8 27	...	9 53	10 47	11 45	12 31	2 11	...	3 35	4 19	5 49	6 42	9 30
Blenheim & Woodstock arr.	8 40	8 40	...		11 ?	12 2	1 23	2 19	...	3 54		6 27	7 0	9 43
Blenheim...ton . . . . dep.	8 11	8 32	...		10 53	11 50	12 38		...	3 42	...		6 48	9 36
Heyford . . . . arr.	8 00	8 33	...		11 0	11 50	12 48		...	3 51			6 59	9 45

		T	MK	MT		M	M			M	M			
	a.m.	a.m.	a.m.	a.m.	a.m.	p.m.	p.m.		p.m.	p.m.	p.m.	p.m.	p.m.	
Heyford . . . . dep		7 55	9 21	9 2		11 25	12 53	..	3 26	..		6 35	8 36	
Bletchington . . . . "	8 6		9 29	9 31		11 32	1 4	..	3 34	..		6 44	8 45	
Blenheim & Woodstock "	7 53		9 25	9 4	9 25	11 24	12 57	2 50	3 18	...	5 37	6 20	8 30	
Kidlington . . . . "	8 15		9 36	9 3	9 41	11 39	1 10	3 0	3 42	4 23	5 55	6 50	8 50	
Wolvercot Halt . . . . "				9 46	9 49		1 19	3 8		4 32	6 4	.	.	
OXFORD . . . . arr.	8 28		9 46	9 3	9 55	11 48	1 28	3 15	3 54	4 38	6 10	7 0	9 0	

K Thursdays excepted.   M Rail Motor Car, one class only.   T Thursdays only.

OXFORD AND SHIPTON.

WEEK DAYS.

	a.m.	n'n.	p.m.	p.m.	p.m.	p.m.	p.m.		a.m.		a.m.	p.m.	p.m.	p.m.	p.m.
OXFORD . . . . dep	8 5	12 0	2 25	3 44	6 15	7 36	8 55	Shipton (for							
Yarnton . . . . . "	8 14	X	.	3 53	R	R	R	Burford) dep	7 57	..	.	12 1	1256	4 47	8 30
Handboro' . . . . . . "	8 22	1215	2 37	4 1	6 26	7 50	9 13	Ascott-under-							
Charlbury . . . . "	8 34	1225	2 48	4 13	6 37	8 1	9 25	Wychwood . "	8 2	...		12 5	.	4 51	8 34
Ascott-under-								Charlbury . . "	8 10	..	1032	12 15	1 5	4 59	8 43
Wychwood . . . "	8 41	1235	.	4 20	...	8 8	9	Handboro' . "	8 21	...	1043	12 27	1 16	5 13	8 56
Shipton (for								Yarnton . . "	R		R	12 35	.	5 20	R
Burford) . . arr.	8 46	1240	2 57	4 25	6 45	8 13	9 36	OXFORD arr	8 33	..	1055	12 45	1 30	5 33	9 10

O Calls to set down Passengers from London and Oxford on notice being given by the Passenger to the Guard at Oxford.   R Passengers from or to Yarnton travel via Oxford.
X Calls to set down Passengers on notice to Guard at Oxford, or to pick up Passengers upon notice being given at the Station before 11.45 a.m.

A TIMETABLE showing the steam railmotor services in the Oxford area in 1909. (Author's Collection)

THE STATION AT AYNHO FOR DEDDINGTON in 1959. The cut off route from Paddington to Birmingham, opened in 1910, can be seen in the background. The 'Down' station building on the left has recently been sold. (J D Edwards)

EX-GREAT WESTERN 2–6–2T NO. 6129 prepares to leave Aynho for Deddington with a stopping service from Oxford to Banbury on 9 September 1964. (F.A. Haynes)

THE TRACK LAYOUT of the flying junction at Aynho in October 1936. The junction connected the new shorter route from Paddington to Birmingham with the original route via Oxford (top left), and was completed and opened on 1 July 1910. (British Railways)

0–4–2T NO. 1453 TOGETHER WITH AUTO-COACH *Thrush* pass Aynho troughs with the 11.05 a.m. service from Banbury to Princes Risborough on 19 May 1962. (Anthony A. Vickers)

'COUNTY' CLASS 4–4–0 NO. 3821 *County of Bedford* passes through Banbury with a 'Down' goods service, c. 1930. (Lens of Sutton)

THIS VIEW OF BANBURY taken in July 1949 shows the rather dilapidated condition of the station's overall roof. Notice also the sign on the platform that advises passengers to change here for the Cheltenham line. (British Railways)

THIS SECOND PICTURE OF BANBURY GENERAL STATION was taken on 18 May 1953, soon after the overall roof was removed. Notice the 'General' added under the station name and the replacement of the Cheltenham branch services notice with 'change here for Eastern Region'. (Author's Collection)

A PORTER looks intently at an oncoming engine as he prepares to carry a large parcel across the tracks at Banbury on 2 November 1955. (British Railways)

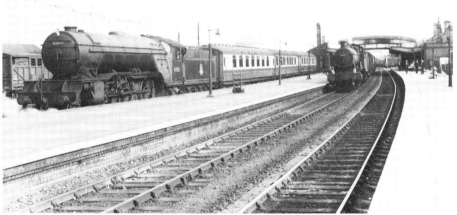

BANBURY STATION on an August day in 1956 with ex-LNER V2 class 60863 on a service to Woodford Halse, and 'Hall' class 6906 *Chicheley Hall* with a 'Down' service unusually pulling into the 'Up' platform. (Real Photos)

BANBURY SHED became part of the Midland Region in 1963 but in this 1964 picture ex-Great Western motive power still predominates. Those identified are, from left to right: 2–8–0 No. 3845 and 'Halls' 6923 *Croxteth Hall* and 7912 *Little Linford Hall*. (T. Longstaff)

'HALL' CLASS NO. 7917 *North Aston Hall*, minus nameplates, being turned at Banbury in the spring of 1963. (M. Soden)

BANBURY MERTON STREET STATION in 1960. (J.D. Edwards)

A SECOND VIEW OF MERTON STREET in 1960 shows what basic facilities were provided here. (J.D. Edwards)

A POSTER announcing the withdrawal of passenger services between Banbury Merton St and Buckingham from 2 January 1961. (J.D. Edwards)

STANDARD CLASS 5 NO. 73010 leaves the Great Central line at Banbury junction with a through service from Sheffield to the South Coast in the summer of 1964. The ex-Great Western main line to Birmingham can be seen on the left. (M. Soden)

The Oxfordshire Ironstone Railway

HUNSLETT ENGINE CO. WORKS NO. 1419, OXFORD IRONSTONE NO. 3 *The President* near Banbury in May 1954. (J.B. Snell)

NO. 170 HUDSWELL CLARKE 0–4–0ST WORKS NO. 1868 *Barabel*, built in 1953, at Wroxton in May 1954. (J.B. Snell)

ANOTHER HUDSWELL CLARK, at Wroxton in May 1954. *Mary*, works No. 1818, was built in 1950. (J.B. Snell)

HORLEY LEVEL CROSSING AND SIGNAL BOX, June 1932. (Oxford University Railway Society Collection)

THE BURSAR shunts at Wroxton in around 1964. (Dr G. Smith)

OXFORD IRONSTONE RAILWAY HUNSLETT 0–6–0 *Spencer* heads a train of ironstone wagons near Wroxton on 25 March 1965. (M. Soden)

HUNSLETT ENGINE CO. 0–6–0 *Frank* works No. 3872, built in 1958, simmers gently at Wroxton. (Dr G. Smith)

THE LARGE ORE CRUSHING PLANT AT WROXTON. (M. Soden)

THIS SMALL SIGNAL CABIN controlled the road crossing at Wroxton. The brick building behind formed part of the company's offices. (M. Soden.)

THE WAGON REPAIR WORKS AT WROXTON. (M. Soden.)

A LINE OF EIGHT REDUNDANT OXFORD IRONSTONE COMPANY LOCOMOTIVES stands at Wroxton on 25 March 1965. (M. Soden)

ACKNOWLEDGEMENTS

I would like to thank the following for their help in providing access to many of the photographs in this book:

The Great Western Trust • Oxfordshire County Libraries •John Edwards
David Castle • Derek Tuck • Bill Turner • Ray Simpson • Mike Soden
Dr Geoff Smith.